14 Reasons
To Roll Your Eyes at Valentine's Day
(But Not at God's Love)

Devotions for When the Only Card in Your Mailbox is a Bill

Pam Kumpe

Scripture quotations from the ESV Bible, The Holy Bible, English Standard Version, copyright 2001 by Crossway Bibles, a publishing ministry of Good News Publishers.

Used by permission. All rights reserved.

No part of this publication may be reproduced, distributed, or transmitted in any form or by any means or stored in a database or retrieval system without prior written permission of the publisher. All rights reserved.

Cover Design by: Pam Kumpe

Copyright 2026 Pam Kumpe

ISBN 979-8-9921326-7-0

*Dedicated to everyone who needs to know they're loved.
And to my late miniature schnauzer, Shelby, who showed
unconditional love for ten years.*

Introduction 1
Why I Wrote This Book

I didn't write this book because I love Valentine's Day. I wrote it because a lot of us... might not love this holiday, depending on our season in life.

Over the years, I've watched this day land like a brick on tender hearts, lonely friends, and people who never thought it might hit so hard.

I've watched singles feel like they're standing outside the candy shop window, noses pressed to the glass. I've watched widows sit through yet another "couples' event" announcement and quietly stare at their hands. I've watched divorced friends flinch at commercials where everything looks perfect, and nobody ever signs papers or packs boxes.

And honestly? I've had my own seasons where February 14 felt less like a celebration and more like a spotlight on what I didn't have.

You know the drill: Everyone's posting flowers, candlelit dinners, sparkly things. You open your mailbox hoping maybe—just maybe—there's something personal in there. Nope. Just a bill, a coupon, and something from the dentist.

Some days, even the mailbox feels like it's mocking you.

So, this little book was born for the women (and a few brave men) who roll their eyes at Valentine's Day and maybe feel a tiny bit guilty about it. This is for the ones who are tired of feeling "less than" because they're not part of a picture-perfect couple strolling through a park holding hands and a small dog.

This is for you if you're single and love Jesus, but this day still stings. Or if you're divorced and you're not sure where you fit anymore. Or if you're widowed and the empty chair is louder than any "I love you" balloon. Or if you're married, but it's complicated, and Valentine's Day feels like one big reminder of what your relationship lacks.

Or you think the whole thing is overhyped—and yet, your heart still aches for something real.

I didn't want to write a book that shook a finger at the world and yelled, "Down with Valentine's," either. I wanted to write a book that quietly sits beside you, nudges your shoulder, and says, "Hey friend, you're not crazy. You're also not unloved."

Because here's the truth: God's love for you is not tied to a calendar date, a relationship status, or a bouquet delivery.

He loved you first. He loves you now. He will love you tomorrow, even after the clearance chocolate is gone and the heart decorations are in the trash.

These 14 devotions are my way of walking with you through the noise of this season and pointing you back to a love that does not wilt, wander, or waver. We're going to roll our eyes at the pressure and the silliness—yes—but then we're going to lift our eyes to Jesus.

You'll find:

- A verse from Scripture (ESV) to anchor each day.
- A short, honest devotional from my heart to yours.
- A simple prayer you can make your own.
- And a little "Love in Action" idea, because one of the best ways to feel loved is to go love somebody else.

You can read one a day for 14 days leading up to Valentine's Day, or anytime you feel ambushed by loneliness, comparison, or that old "not enough" lie.

You can read them in your favorite chair with a mug in your hand, in your car between errands, or late at night under the covers when the world is quiet and your thoughts are loud.

I hope that as you turn these pages, you'll feel seen. That you'll laugh a little. Maybe cry a bit. But most of all, that you'll remember you are not the leftover, the extra, or the one God somehow forgot to write into the love story.

Friend, you are already chosen and already wanted. Already loved with an everlasting love that doesn't come with an expiration date or a gift receipt.

So, if the only card in your mailbox is a bill, if your phone isn't buzzing with romantic plans, if you're somewhere between hopeful and heartache—this book is for you.

Let's roll our eyes at Valentine's Day together.

But not at God's love.

Never at His love.

Pam Kumpe

Day 1
Love Didn't Start with Cupid

"We love because He first loves us.
1 John 4:19, ESV

If Valentine's Day makes you want to roll your eyes so hard you see last week, you're not alone.

The world acts like love showed up when someone invented heart-shaped candy and awkward red teddy bears. But long before Cupid ever missed his first shot, God loved you. His love isn't a feeling that comes and goes with hormones and holidays. His love is the starting line.

When no one texts back, when the mailbox only delivers bills, when the restaurant host asks, "Table for just one?"— remember, you are not an afterthought. You are loved first, best, and forever by the God who made you on purpose.

So, if you need to roll your eyes today, roll them at the commercials, at the pressure, at the cultural nonsense. But not at the cross. That's where Love stepped into our mess and said, "I choose you," before you ever chose Him.

Prayer:

Lord, thank You that Your love came first. When I feel overlooked or unwanted, remind me that my story doesn't begin with romance; it starts with You. Help me rest in the truth that I am already loved, already seen, and already chosen. Amen.

Love in Action:

Write one person a quick message that simply says, "God loved us first, and I'm grateful He put you in my life."

Day 2
God Doesn't Wait for February 14

"The steadfast love of the LORD never ceases;
his mercies never come to an end."
Lamentations 3:22, ESV

Valentine's Day is one date on a calendar. God's love is not.

I've had days when I wanted to circle a date and say, "Okay God, show up big here." But He doesn't limit Himself to the days we decorate with hearts. His mercies roll in new every morning—not just the ones with chocolate sales attached.

If today feels loud with expectations, remember: God's love met you yesterday. It will greet you tomorrow. And it's covering you right now—whether you're in your pajamas or at your desk.

The world offers one day of glitter. God provides a lifetime of faithfulness. You don't have to wait for a holiday to feel worthy of attention from Heaven. His eyes are on you on ordinary Tuesdays, long workdays, and quiet evenings when no one knows you're lonely but Him.

Prayer:

Father, thank You that Your love doesn't run on a holiday schedule. I'm grateful that Your mercies meet me in the middle of my everyday life. Help me notice Your presence in the simple, overlooked moments today. Amen.

Love in Action:

Do one tiny surprise today on a totally "ordinary" task—like leaving a sticky note with a Bible verse on the bathroom mirror or in a lunch sack.

Day 3
Roses Wilt, Grace Doesn't

> *"The grass withers, the flower fades, but the Word of our God will stand forever."*
> *Isaiah 40:8, ESV*

Those pretty red roses? Give them a week, and they'll be drooping over the edge of the vase as they stayed up too late.

Most of what the world calls "love" posts well on social media, and then fades, leaving petals on the table and a mess on the floor.

God's love isn't like that. His promises don't wilt. His faithfulness doesn't dry up. His grace doesn't brown around the edges. When people change their minds, walk away, or grow distant, the Word of our God still stands.

The most excellent fragrance ever offered to you happened on a cross and was confirmed by an empty tomb. So let the roses fade. God's love, that holds you, will still be alive and strong tomorrow.

Prayer:

Lord, thank You that Your love does not fade like flowers. When I chase temporary things, gently pull me back to what lasts—Your Word, Your grace, and Your heart for me. Amen.

Love in Action:

Give someone *non*-flower encouragement: text a verse, send a voice memo prayer, or share one way you see God at work in them.

Day 4
Single is Not Synonymous with Unloved

> *"I praise you, for I am fearfully and wonderfully made."*
> Psalm 139:14, ESV

If I could sit across from you with a cup of something warm, I'd look you in the eye and say this slowly: your relationship status is not your value.

Being single, divorced, widowed, or "it's complicated" doesn't automatically stamp unwanted across your story. Sometimes the culture acts like the only people who win on Valentine's Day are the ones holding hands at the restaurant. But Heaven is not handing out trophies based on who got a reservation.

You were fearfully and wonderfully made before any date, ring, breakup, or heartbreak. God's delight in you did not begin when someone noticed you—and it certainly doesn't end when someone leaves.

You are not the last pick. You are a woman (or man) created with intention by a God who sees every detail and calls you precious.

Prayer:

Father, when I'm tempted to tie my value to my relationship status, remind me that I am fearfully and wonderfully made. Help me to see myself the way You see me—deeply loved and never as a second choice. Amen.

Love in Action:

Encourage a single friend (or widow, or divorced friend) with a specific compliment that has nothing to do with looks—something about their character.

Day 5
When the Only Card in Your Mailbox is a Bill

"The LORD is near to the brokenhearted and saves the crushed in spirit."
Psalm 34:18, ESV

I've opened the mailbox before, half-hoping some surprise card or kind note would be waiting—only to find a bill staring back at me like, "Hey, remember me?"

Maybe that's your reality, too. No pink envelopes. No love notes. Just utilities and junk mail.

Here's the thing: God doesn't send His love in cardstock with glitter. He sends it in nearness. When your spirit feels crushed, He moves closer, not farther away.

Your heartache is not invisible to Him. The broken places in you are not places He avoids; they're places He visits. The Lord is near the brokenhearted—not just the cheerful, put-together, Instagram-ready.

If your mailbox is full of bills, your life can still be full of His presence. Heaven is not indifferent to your tears. God sees. And God knows.

Prayer:

Lord, when the emptiness feels loud, and my heart feels bruised, draw near. Remind me that You, Lord, see me. Be close to me in the places that hurt. Amen.

Love in Action:

Mail or hand-deliver a simple handwritten note or card to someone who wouldn't expect it—no holiday needed, just "thinking of you."

Day 6
God Sends Better Love Notes

"I have loved you with an everlasting love; therefore, I have continued my faithfulness."
Jeremiah 31:3, ESV

I love a good handwritten note. But even the sweetest card eventually gets tucked into a drawer or lost in a move.

God's love notes are different. They're not limited to one holiday aisle. His Word is a whole bookcase full of, "I am with you," "I will not leave you," and "I love you more than you can imagine."

When you open Scripture, you're not reading a dry manual; you're hearing the heart of Someone who has loved you with an everlasting love. Not a trial run. Not a "we'll see how this goes." Everlasting.

On a day when everyone else is chasing something shiny, what if you opened your Bible and asked, "Lord, remind me again how You feel about me"? I promise—He'll answer.

The world offers cards that come and go. God offers a covenant that doesn't break.

Prayer:

Father, thank You for the love story written in Your Word. Give me a fresh hunger to open my Bible and hear Your heart for me. Let Your promises be louder than my insecurities today. Amen.

Love in Action:

Write out today's verse on an index card and tuck it somewhere someone will find it—inside a book, break room, church bathroom, laundry room.

Day 7
You're Allowed to be Sad Today

"You have kept count of my tossings; put my tears in your bottle. Are they not in your book?"
Psalm 56:8, ESV

Can we just say it? Some Valentine's Days hurt.

Maybe you're grieving someone you loved. Perhaps you're staring at the ruins of a relationship that didn't survive. Maybe the day pokes a bruise you wish would finally stop aching.

You don't have to slap a fake smile over real pain. God is not impressed by your pretending. Your honesty moves him. He keeps count of your restless nights. He cares enough to notice every single tear.

If the world's saying, "Love is in the air!" and you're thinking, "Well, not at my house," you're not a bad Christian. You're a real human with a tender heart in a broken world. Jesus knows what grief feels like. He's not ashamed of your sadness.

So, if today needs to be a day of tears more than chocolate, that's okay. Let them fall in the presence of a God who catches them.

Prayer:

Jesus, You know what it is to be a Man of Sorrows. When my heart is heavy, sit with me in the middle of it. Help me bring my grief to You instead of hiding it. Hold me close when I feel fragile. Amen.

Love in Action:

Reach out to someone who might be grieving—send a short "You're on my heart today. I'm praying for you" text and actually pray.

Day 8
Love is a Command, not a Card

"A new commandment I give to you, that you love one another."
John 13:34, ESV

Valentine's Day asks, "Who's loving you?" Jesus asks, "Who are you loving?"

That shift changes everything. Instead of measuring our worth by who sends us flowers, we start looking around for who needs encouragement, a kind word, or a simple act of care. Love moves from performance to practice.

I've discovered that some of my loneliest days turned around when I stopped asking, "Why doesn't anyone notice me?" and started praying, "Lord, who can I notice today?" A text. A handwritten note. A cookie dropped off at someone's door—a homeless friend given a fresh pair of socks or a warm meal.

Love as a command means I don't have to *feel* super romantic to obey it. I just have to be willing. Jesus didn't say, "Wait until you're adored," but "Love one another as I have loved you."

Prayer:
Lord, don't let me get stuck staring at my own emptiness. Open my eyes to someone who needs Your love today. Help me love others the way You've loved me—on ordinary days, with ordinary kindness. Amen.

Day 9
God Already Knows Your Love Story

"Trust in the LORD with all your heart, and do not lean on your own understanding."
Proverbs 3:5, ESV

I like to know the plan. Don't you?

When it comes to relationships, we make timelines in our heads: "By this age, I'll be married. By the end of this season, things will be healed. By this date, I'll feel whole again." And when real life refuses to cooperate, we panic.

But here's the comfort: God is not confused about your story. He's not scrolling through your life thinking, "Oh no, I didn't see that coming." He knows the people who will walk in, and the ones who will walk out, and the grace He'll pour over both.

Trusting Him with all your heart doesn't mean you stop caring or desiring; it means you stop trying to do His job.

If Valentine's Day makes you feel behind schedule, hand that imaginary calendar back to the Lord. Let Him write at His pace. He's very good at redemption.

Prayer:

Father, I confess I often lean on my own understanding, especially in relationships. Take my timelines, my fears, and my hopes, and hold them in Your wise hands. Amen.

Love in Action:

Share a short testimony with someone about a time God wrote a better ending than you expected, even if it took a while.

Day 10
Friendship is Real Love Too

"For if they fall, one will lift up his fellow."
Ecclesiastes 4:10, ESV

Sometimes the sweetest love in your life isn't romantic—it's the friend who shows up with coffee when you're tired, or the one who texts, "You on my heart today."

Valentine's Day can make friendship feel like the consolation prize, but Scripture treats it as a gift. We were never meant to walk alone. God designed us to need encouragers, truth-tellers, laugh-until-you-snort buddies, and "I'm-praying-for-you" sisters and brothers.

So, if you're not going on a date, maybe this is the year you celebrate friendship on purpose. Send a silly meme. Invite someone over for soup. Write a note to the person who lifted you when you were falling apart.

You may not have a romantic dinner reservation, but you might have a friend who has stood beside you through thick and thin. That's real love, too. Don't underestimate it.

Be that friend for someone who could use your company and a lift in return.

Prayer:

Lord, thank You for the gift of friends who lift me when I fall. Please show me how to cherish and nurture those relationships. Amen.

Love in Action:

Pick one friend and send them one specific memory that makes you smile and say, "I'm thankful for you because..."

Day 11
Already Chosen

"He chose us in him before the foundation of the world."
Ephesians 1:4, ESV

Some of us carry old playground memories—the ones where teams were picked, and we stood there, waiting, heart sinking, wondering if we'd be chosen last.

Valentine's Day can stir that same feeling. Everyone else seems picked and paired up. And you feel like the kid still standing on the sidelines. But long before any of that, before the world even spun on its axis, God chose you in Christ. You were selected in love, on purpose.

Being chosen by God doesn't guarantee an easy or romantic road. But it does guarantee this: you are wanted. Your name is known. Your heart is seen.

So, when the old lies whisper, remember, you were chosen before the foundation of the world.

Prayer:

Father, when rejection stings, or memories rise, let this truth anchor me—You wanted me before anyone else had an opinion. Amen.

Love in Action:

Tell someone younger in the faith—or someone who struggles with insecurity— "You are not an accident. God chose you on purpose."

Day 12
Quiet Love Counts Too

"Love bears all things, believes all things, hopes all things, endures all things."
1 Corinthians 13:7, ESV

Not all love looks like grand gestures and sparkling photos. Some of the most authentic love is quiet.

It's the spouse who keeps praying when marriage is hard. The adult child who calls her aging parent. The friend who answers the late-night text. The church member who slips a grocery card to a struggling family.

These acts don't trend online, but Heaven sees them. Don't discount the quiet ways you can show up—listening, encouraging, serving, forgiving. Those things matter. They reflect the heart of Jesus far more than a one-day display.

And if you long for someone to love you like that, remember: God already does. His love is steady, not flashy. He has been quietly carrying you longer than you know.

Prayer:

Lord, help me value the quiet, enduring kind of love more than temporary fireworks. Amen.

Love in Action:

Do one quiet, unseen act of kindness today and *don't* tell anyone, just you and Jesus: chores for someone, a small gift, a task you take off their plate.

Day 13
Turn Valentine's Day into a Mission Day

"...through love serve one another."
Galatians 5:13, ESV

If the day feels empty, here's a radical idea: fill it by serving someone else.

What if Valentine's became the day you bring cookies to the shelter, handwritten notes to nurses, or snacks to the woman at the laundromat? What if instead of wondering who will love you well today, you asked Jesus to show you who needs His love through you?

I've watched hardened faces soften over a simple sandwich and a kind word on the street. I've seen eyes fill with tears when someone realizes, "You remembered me." Those moments remind me: love is not a spectator sport. It's a mission.

You don't need a fancy budget. A smile, a listening ear, a verse scribbled on an index card can carry more weight than expensive roses.

When we serve through love, we end up feeling less alone, because we bump right into the heart of God—He is always moving toward the hurting.

Prayer:

Jesus, show me someone I can bless today. Turn my loneliness into compassion. Use my hands, my words, and my small offerings to remind someone else that they are not forgotten. Amen.

Love in Action:

Prepare a small "love bundle": a snack, a drink, or a hygiene item, and keep it in your car or bag, ready to give to someone in need.

Day 14
Messiah

"For the marriage of the Lamb has come, and his Bride has made herself ready."
Revelation 19:7, ESV

The best love story doesn't end with a proposal in a restaurant. It ends with a wedding in glory.

Scripture tells us there is a day coming when all of God's people—the Bride of Christ—will be gathered with Jesus at the marriage supper of the Lamb. No one will be left out because they weren't pretty enough, young enough, or *couple* enough. The invitation rests on the blood of Christ, not our charm.

That means, if you are in Christ, you are headed toward a celebration bigger than your imagination. No heartbreak, no divorce papers, no diagnosis, no lonely holiday can cancel that future.

So, when Valentine's Day makes your hope feel small, lift your eyes. This is not the final chapter. There is a feast ahead, a Bridegroom who cannot fail, and a joy no one can take from you.

Prayer:

Lord Jesus, thank You that my final destination is a wedding, not a wasteland. When I feel left out here, remind me that I am part of Your Bride, loved and welcomed forever. Keep my hope anchored in what's coming. Amen.

Love in Action:

Encourage another believer with a *future hope* reminder—send Revelation 19:7 or another verse and say, "We're headed to a wedding, friend."

Closing Devotional
You Are Loved on Ordinary Days, Too

> "Surely goodness and mercy shall follow me all
> the days of my life..."
> Psalm 23:6, ESV

Valentine's Day comes and goes in a noisy swirl of red and pink, and then... It's Tuesday again, year after year.

And for some, there are no balloons. No big gestures. No themed displays at the grocery store, calling them by name.

Just laundry, dishes, emails, traffic, and trying to decide what's for supper—again. Or sitting with a sick one. Or no one. Or it could just be you, all alone.

But here's what I want you to remember as we close this little book: God's love is not a high-holiday event. It's a daily reality. His goodness and mercy don't follow you on special occasions only; they follow you **all the days** of your life.

The loud ones. The lonely ones. The "nothing special happened today" ones. You are loved when you're strong and when you're spent. You are loved when you're laughing and when you're numb. You are loved on the big days and the boring days, too.

Prayer:

Lord, thank You that Your love doesn't depend on a holiday, a mood, or my performance. Amen.

Love in Action:

Do one small, ordinary act of kindness today. Surprise someone. Do it with Christ's love. And repeat the other 364 days of the year.

Truths About God's Love

1. God Loved You First
Before you reached for God, He reached for you.

2. God's Love Is Everlasting
His love doesn't expire, fade, or give up

3. Nothing Can Separate You from His Love
No mistake, no present struggle puts you out of His reach.

4. God's Love Is Steadfast and Endures Forever
His love is not seasonal; it's steady and unshakable.

5. God's Love Is Personal and Knowing
He doesn't love you in a vague, general way—He knows your name and every detail of your life.

6. God Showed His Love at the Cross
The cross is the once-for-all proof that you are loved beyond measure.

7. God's Love Is a Refuge in Trouble
When life falls apart, His love becomes your safe place and shelter.

8. God's Love Adopts You into His Family

In Christ, you're not just tolerated; you are welcomed as His child.

9. God's Love Is Merciful and Compassionate

He meets you with compassion, not condemnation, when you fail.

10. God's Love Is Faithful on Your Worst Days

Even when you are faithless, He remains faithful.

11. God's Love Is Perfect and Casts Out Fear

His perfect love speaks peace to anxious hearts and fearful minds.

12. God's Love Is with You Wherever You Go

You are never outside the reach of His presence or His care.

13. God's Love Is Better Than Life

His love satisfies the deepest hunger of your soul.

14. God's Love Will Never Let You Go

If you belong to Jesus, His love holds you fast now and forever.

Walk with Me

When Valentine's Day Feels Like High School All Over Again

> *"Fear not, for I have redeemed you; I have called you by name, you are mine."*
> Isaiah 43:1, ESV

In high school, I somehow ended up in a group called the *Purple Pride Angels*—a dozen girls chosen to work the football games. We handed out programs, helped with the chains, paraded around with water bottles, and posed for the yearbook in white go-go boots, purple hot pants, and lighter purple tops. (Whoa! Scary to think of me like that, I know.)

Truly, nothing says *future trauma* like hot pants and a zoomed-in yearbook photo.

And that group didn't make me more popular.

If anything, it painted a bigger target on my back. We were labeled snooty and a few other choice words.

I was quiet back then, an introvert in costume, and suddenly I was a spectacle. People saw the outfit—not the girl wearing it.

I used to tease my twin that I only made the group because she'd dated half the football team, since she was friendly and outgoing, and the boys were confused about which twin they were voting for. (With us looking so much alike, that logic tracked.)

But underneath the jokes, I remember the ache. I didn't want the spotlight; I wanted belonging—the quieter version with less spotlight.

So yes, Valentine's Day can feel like high school all over again.

For years, that holiday brought back flashbacks—times when I wanted to be alone. Because, yes, I could be lonely, even in a room full of people, or on the sidelines at a football game.

But somewhere along the way, God began to redeem "alone" for me.

As a writer, I've found that being alone with my notebook and my Bible no longer feels like rejection. It's like an invitation. I've found my team in words—stories, sentences, prayers, pages, books—and most of all, in the One who calls Himself the Word.

No more hot pants. Or go-go boots!

These days, being alone can be holy. Sure, lonely still visits sometimes, sure. But alone with Jesus? That's different. That's where I remember I am already chosen, already known, already loved. Not for my go-go boots, not for my performance, not for my place on some high school list, but because He has called me by name.

So, if Valentine's Day drags you back to those awful high school memories—or any trauma-inducing holiday—awkward, exposed, left out (but somehow in)—hear this: you are not that girl (boy) anymore. And even then, even in the purple hot pants days, God saw the quiet soul inside the costume.

And He gave me a voice. Hope. Joy. And His love. He still does.

Books by Pam Kumpe

Annie Grace Kree Chronicles Series
1 Untied Shoelace
2 Unknown Soul
3 Rescue of Undaunted Spirit
4 Unwanted Sidekick
5 Unwavering Hope
6 Unshackled Courage

Other Novels
Rescue at Three Sisters Springs
Looking for Daddy's Girl
Summertime Sprinkler
Where Horses Run Secrets Hide

Devotional
Looking for Daddy's Girl Devotional
See You in the Funny Papers
A Scoop of Inspiration
You Are Not a Typo
A 25-Day Countdown to Christmas

Bible Study
Think Outside the Pit Devotional
Think Outside the Pit Workbook

Children
In the Lick of Time
A Goat with a Tote
Hattie Holmes Holds Her Breath
Hattie and Mattie! Oh, They Love the Bunny!
Cranky Camel and the Candy Cane Caper
Cranky the Camel and Max Go to School
Cranky the Camel and Barnyard's Got Talent
Spike's Glow

Rehab Ministry Devotionals
Things I Learned in Jail
From Court to Christ

Homeless Ministry
My View from the Bridge
My View from the Street
My View of the Heart

You Are Lost Series
Book One: The Mystery of Sneaky Pants
Book Two: The Mystery of Sneaky Paws
Book Three: The Mystery of the Sneaky Parrots
Book Four: The Mystery of Sneaky Dill Pickens
Parrots, Pranks, and Prayers Devotional

www.pamkumpe.com

www.ingramcontent.com/pod-product-compliance
Lightning Source LLC
Chambersburg PA
CBHW070452050426
42450CB00012B/3247